The INSIDE GUIDE

MOVEMENTS FOR EQUALITY

The Story of the

Women's Suffrage
Movement

By Jennifer Lombardo

Cavendish
Square

Published in 2024 by Cavendish Square Publishing, LLC
2544 Clinton Street Buffalo, NY 14224

Website: cavendishsq.com

This publication represents the opinions and views of the author based on their personal experience, knowledge, and research. The information in this book serves as a general guide only. The author and publisher have used their best efforts in preparing this book and disclaim liability rising directly or indirectly from the use and application of this book.

Disclaimer: Portions of this work were originally authored by Jill Keppeler and published as *Women's Suffrage Movement* (Civic Participation: Working for Civil Rights). All new material this edition authored by Jennifer Lombardo.

All websites were available and accurate when this book was sent to press.

Cataloging-in-Publication Data

Names: Lombardo, Jennifer.
Title: The story of the women's suffrage movement / Jennifer Lombardo.
Description: Buffalo, New York: Cavendish Square Publishing, 2024. | Series: The inside guide: movements for equality | Includes glossary, index, and bibliographic information
Identifiers: ISBN 9781502668165 (pbk) | ISBN 9781502668172 (library bound) | ISBN 9781502668189 (ebook)
Subjects: LCSH: Suffrage–Juvenile literature | Voting–Juvenile literature | Women's rights–Juvenile literature
Classification: LCC JF851 L66 2024 | DDC 324.6–dc24

Editor: Jennifer Lombardo
Copyeditor: Michele Suchomel-Casey
Designer: Deanna Paternostro

The photographs in this book are used by permission and through the courtesy of: Cover, pp. 4, 7, 14, 15, 16, 22, 29 (left and right) Everett Collection/Shutterstock.com; p. 8 File:Mary Wollstonecraft by John Opie(c. 1797).jpg/Wikimedia Commons; p. 10 Alizada Studios/Shutterstock.com; p. 12 File:Women's Rights Convention attendees.jpg/Wikimedia Commons; p. 19 Lefteris Papaulakis/Shutterstock.com; p. 20 Cinematic Collection/Alamy Stock Photo; p. 25 File:Smithsonian - NPG - Zitkala-Sa -NPG.2006.10.jpg/Wikimedia Commons; p. 27 File:RochesterNYAnthonyGraveElectionDay2020A.jpg/Wikimedia Commons; p. 29 (center) Ink Drop/Shutterstock.com.

Some of the images in this book illustrate individuals who are models. The depictions do not imply actual situations or events.

CPSIA compliance information: Batch #CSCSQ24: For further information contact Cavendish Square Publishing LLC at 1-877-980-4450.

Printed in the United States of America

Find us on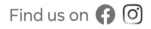

CONTENTS

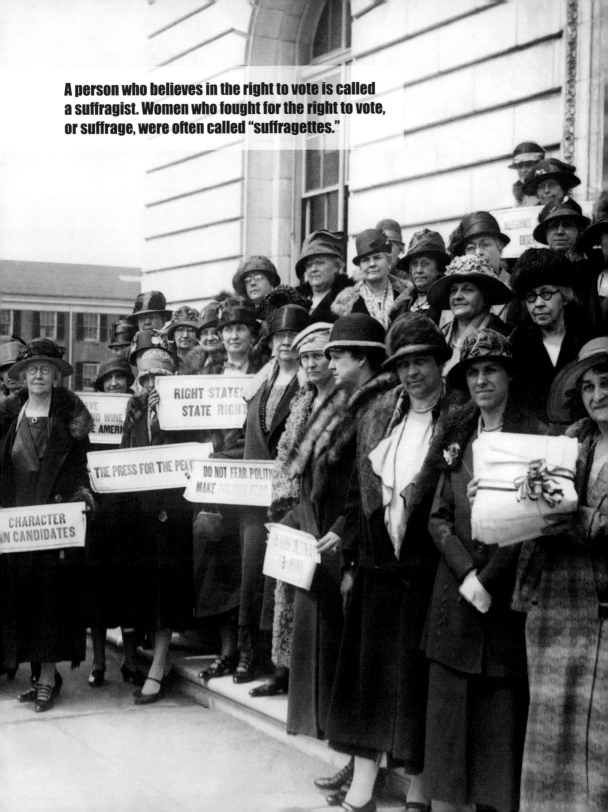

A person who believes in the right to vote is called a suffragist. Women who fought for the right to vote, or suffrage, were often called "suffragettes."

SECOND-CLASS CITIZENS

From the earliest days of the United States, women were second-class citizens. This means that they were not given the same rights and opportunities as men. Because the Founding Fathers based the laws they wrote on the laws England had at the time, women were not allowed to divorce their husband, serve on a jury, vote, or do many other things that most men were automatically allowed to do. Today, thanks to the brave and tireless actions of **activists**, American women have all of these rights. Gaining voting rights was an especially tough fight.

An International Movement

The fight for women's suffrage in the United States grew from a larger, international struggle for women's rights. In the early days of the United States, there were many **stereotypes**

Fast Fact

The view that women shouldn't work outside the home applied only to white women. Women of color were expected to work when they were enslaved. After slavery ended, they often took jobs as housekeepers and nannies for wealthy white women.

WHY DOES VOTING MATTER?

In the United States today, all citizens have the legal right to vote once they turn 18. However, as many as half don't show up to the polls. In some cases, this is due to **voter suppression** laws that mainly affect poor people and people of color. In other cases, people may not vote because they don't like their choices.

About 15 percent of American citizens choose not to vote because they believe their vote doesn't matter. However, experts say this is false. Voting is one of the best ways for citizens to create change in their country. If voting did nothing, voter suppression would not exist, and no one would ever have had to fight for their right to vote.

and expectations about women's place in society. However, many American women began to reject the idea that their only true purpose was to be wives, mothers, and homemakers. They were interested in being a real part of society and making a difference.

In the 1800s, there were many **reform** groups whose members wanted to change society for the better. Many American women wanted to be involved—and to be taken seriously while they did so. They worked with women in

Fast Fact
Activists saw voting as the first step toward equal rights. Using their right to vote, they could change laws that were keeping women and people of color **oppressed**.

In many places around the world, women have historically been expected to stay at home, have many children, and keep their opinions to themselves. Even today, some people believe this is the way women should behave.

In 1792, a British woman named Mary Wollstonecraft [*shown here*] published *A Vindication of the Rights of Women*, which called for women to have the same rights as men. Her daughter, Mary Wollstonecraft Shelley, wrote the world's first science fiction book, *Frankenstein*.

other countries, writing letters to each other and holding meetings to exchange ideas about how to achieve their goal of women's suffrage.

According to the National Parks Service (NPS), American suffragettes were inspired by revolutions in not only their own country, but also in France, Haiti, Mexico, and Russia. **Immigrants** from these countries brought ideals of freedom and political **agency** to the United States and helped advance the cause.

The First Step

Some of the women who would lead the U.S. women's suffrage movement were first involved in the abolitionist movement, which sought to end slavery in the United States. However, some abolitionist groups didn't accept female members, and the ones that did often kept women out of leadership **roles**. Two sisters named Angelina and Sarah Moore Grimké were criticized because they made speeches against slavery to groups that contained both men and women.

Fast Fact

Abolitionism and women's suffrage were strongly tied together, but racism from some white suffragettes often made it difficult for both movements to advance.

In 1840, abolitionists Lucretia Mott and Elizabeth Cady Stanton traveled to London, England, for the World Anti-Slavery Convention—but they and other women were forced to watch instead of actually taking part. Mott, Stanton, and many other women came to the conclusion that to be taken seriously as reformers, they first needed the right to vote.

Today, the building where the Seneca Falls Convention was held is a museum that people can visit.

GETTING STARTED

Many people mark the beginning of the U.S. women's suffrage movement as July 1848, when the first U.S. women's rights convention took place in Seneca Falls, New York. More than 200 people attended the event, which Mott and Stanton organized.

During the convention, Stanton read out loud from a document called the Declaration of Sentiments. It outlined the rights that women were seeking. About half of the people who attended the convention—68 women and 32 men—signed the document to show their support for women's rights. The convention also produced 12 resolutions, or goals. One of these called for women's suffrage. Many thought this particular resolution should be removed, but Stanton argued in its favor. After famous abolitionist Frederick Douglass gave a speech supporting women's suffrage, the resolution stayed.

Fast Fact

Ancient Greece and Rome were two of the world's earliest democracies—a form of government where citizens elect their leaders. However, women were not given the vote in these places. Only men who owned property could vote.

Our Roll of Honor

Containing all the
Signatures to the "Declaration of Sentiments"
Set Forth by the First

Woman's Rights Convention,

held at
Seneca Falls, New York
July 19-20, 1848

LADIES:

Lucretia Mott	Sophronia Taylor	Rachel D. Bonnel
Harriet Cady Eaton	Cynthia Davis	Betsey Tewksbury
Margaret Pryor	Hannah Plant	Rhoda Palmer
Elizabeth Cady Stanton	Lucy Jones	Margaret Jenkins
Eunice Newton Foote	Sarah Whitney	Cynthia Fuller
Mary Ann M'Clintock	Mary H. Hallowell	Mary Martin
Margaret Schooley	Elizabeth Conklin	P. A. Culvert
Martha C. Wright	Sally Pitcher	Susan R. Doty
Jane C. Hunt	Mary Conklin	Rebecca Race
Amy Post	Susan Quinn	Sarah A. Mosher
Catherine F. Stebbins	Mary S. Mirror	Mary E. Vail
Mary Ann Frink	Phebe King	Lucy Spalding
Lydia Mount	Julia Ann Drake	Lovina Latham
Delia Mathews	Charlotte Woodward	Sarah Smith
Catherine C. Paine	Martha Underhill	Eliza Martin
Elizabeth W. M'Clintock	Dorothy Mathews	Maria E. Wilbur
Malvina Seymour	Eunice Barker	Elizabeth D. Smith
Phebe Mosher	Sarah R. Woods	Caroline Barker
Catherine Shaw	Lydia Gild	Ann Porter
Deborah Scott	Sarah Hoffman	Experience Gibbs
Sarah Hallowell	Elizabeth Leslie	Antoinette E. Segur
Mary M'Clintock	Martha Ridley	Hannah J. Latham
Mary Gilbert		Sarah Sisson

GENTLEMEN:

Richard P. Hunt	William S. Dell	Nathan J. Milliken
Samuel D. Tillman	James Mott	S. E. Woodworth
Justin Williams	William Burroughs	Edward F. Underhill
Elisha Foote	Robert Smallbridge	George W. Pryor
Frederick Douglass	Jacob Mathews	Joel Bunker
Henry W. Seymour	Charles L. Hoskins	Isaac VanTassel
Henry Seymour	Thomas M'Clintock	Thomas Dell
David Spalding	Saron Phillips	E. W. Capron
William G. Barker	Jacob P. Chamberlain	Stephen Shear
Elias J. Doty	Jonathan Metcalf	Henry Hatley
John Jones		Azaliah Schooley

This card lists the names of the people who signed the Declaration of Sentiments.

WOMEN AGAINST VOTING

At the time the Declaration of Sentiments was written, many people—even many women—thought women were too emotional to be trusted with something as important as voting. They also claimed society would fall apart if women were able to do things outside the home.

Women who were against female suffrage generally already had high status and some political power because of the men they were married to. The system benefited them, but if all women were allowed to vote, they knew many of them would vote in ways these women didn't agree with. To try to keep that from happening, some created Anti-Suffrage Leagues to work against the suffragettes.

Organizing Events

After the Seneca Falls convention, organizers started to plan many more women's rights conventions. The first National Women's Rights Convention took place in October 1850 in Worcester, Massachusetts. It was organized by Paulina Wright Davis and other suffragists.

The event featured **debates**, speakers, and plans for the future of the movement. More than 1,000 people attended. While participants talked about many topics, suffrage was a main focus. For some time after this, national women's rights conventions were held every year.

However, just as the women's suffrage movement was really getting started, the American Civil War began in 1861. Many who took part in the suffrage movement refocused their energy on helping the war effort.

Susan B. Anthony is one of the best-known suffragettes, but many women—and even some men—worked hard to bring about women's suffrage.

Splitting the Party

After the Civil War ended in 1865, women were ready to get back to work for suffrage. In 1866, Stanton and Susan B. Anthony started the American Equal Rights Association (AERA), which was dedicated to gaining voting rights for all.

The organization soon ran into a problem. Many of those who fought for women's suffrage were against any amendment that gave formerly enslaved men the right to vote but did not also give that right to women. Others, such as Frederick Douglass, thought it was more important for Black men to earn the right to vote first and that women could fight for their own rights in a separate amendment.

Ultimately, this is what happened: The 15th Amendment granted Black men the right to vote in 1869, while the 19th Amendment, granting women the right to vote, wasn't passed until 1919. Despite their background as

Fast Fact

Frances Ellen Watkins Harper was a Black woman who criticized both Black male suffragists and white female suffragists for not working together. She pointed out that both sides ignored Black women.

abolitionists, Stanton, Anthony, and others refused to work to get the 15th Amendment ratified, or formally approved.

In 1869, the AERA split over this issue. Stanton and Anthony formed the National Woman Suffrage Association. Other suffragists formed the American Woman Suffrage Association.

Same Goal, Different Methods

The members of the National Woman Suffrage Association, which was based in New York State, devoted themselves to working toward a women's suffrage amendment to the U.S. Constitution. The members of the American Woman Suffrage Association, which was based in Boston, Massachusetts, worked toward changing laws at the state level.

This split did not help their cause. Instead, it divided the supporters, their message, and the money they had available to work with. In 1890, the two groups reunited, forming the National American Woman Suffrage Association. The cause began to gain ground again.

Fast Fact

Women were allowed to vote in Wyoming starting in 1869—before it was a state. Wyoming refused to officially join the United States unless women were allowed to keep their right to vote.

Ida B. Wells (*shown here*) and Sojourner Truth were two Black women who fought tirelessly for abolition and women's suffrage.

President Woodrow Wilson finally passed the law that gave women the vote after suffragettes spent two years of his presidential term protesting against his inaction.

CIVIL DISOBEDIENCE

One tool suffragettes used in their fight was civil disobedience. This means breaking laws to make a political point. For example, even though it was illegal, Susan B. Anthony and 15 other women voted in the U.S. election of 1872, during which President Ulysses S. Grant was running for re-election against Horace Greeley. Anthony voted for Grant and was arrested. She went to trial and fought the charges but was fined $100 ($2,465 in today's money)—which she refused to pay.

The suffragettes' ultimate goal was female suffrage at the federal, or national, level. This would make women's suffrage legal in every state at the same time. While they were working toward that goal, a few states began to approve women's suffrage on their own. By 1900, Colorado, Utah, Wyoming, and Idaho had all given women the right to vote.

Fast Fact

Anthony dared the judge in her case to send her to prison. He refused because he knew that would allow her to **appeal** her case to the Supreme Court, which might decide in her favor.

The Next Generation

The early members of the women's suffrage movement grew old before they achieved their goal.

RUNNING FOR OFFICE

Even though women did not yet have the right to vote, the Equal Rights Party nominated Victoria Woodhull for president in the 1872 election. No one is sure how many votes she received. Belva Lockwood ran for president in the 1884 and 1888 elections. She received more than 4,000 votes in 1884. Lockwood was also the first female lawyer to argue in front of the U.S. Supreme Court.

Female candidates have come a long way since then, but they are still not equally represented. In 2023, Congress had a record high of 150 female members. However, that number still represents only about 25 percent of Congress. In 2020, Kamala Harris became the first female U.S. vice president, but as of 2023, there has never been a female president.

Lucretia Mott died in 1880, followed by Elizabeth Cady Stanton in 1902 and Susan B. Anthony in 1906.

However, new women stepped up to lead the suffrage movement. Carrie Chapman Catt took over the National American Woman Suffrage Association in 1900. Alice Paul, an American woman who had studied in England and helped

Fast Fact

The 19th Amendment was first proposed, or put forward for a vote, in 1878. It was reintroduced and rejected every year for the next 41 years.

This stamp from 1948 celebrated 100 years since the Seneca Falls Convention.

with the suffrage campaign there, started the National Women's Party in 1913.

As new leaders continued the fight, more states approved suffrage rights for women. By 1918, 11 more states, including California and New York, had given women full voting rights.

Facing Violence

When Alice Paul returned to the United States and started the National Women's Party, she brought with her methods used by the more **militant** women's suffrage movement in England. The American

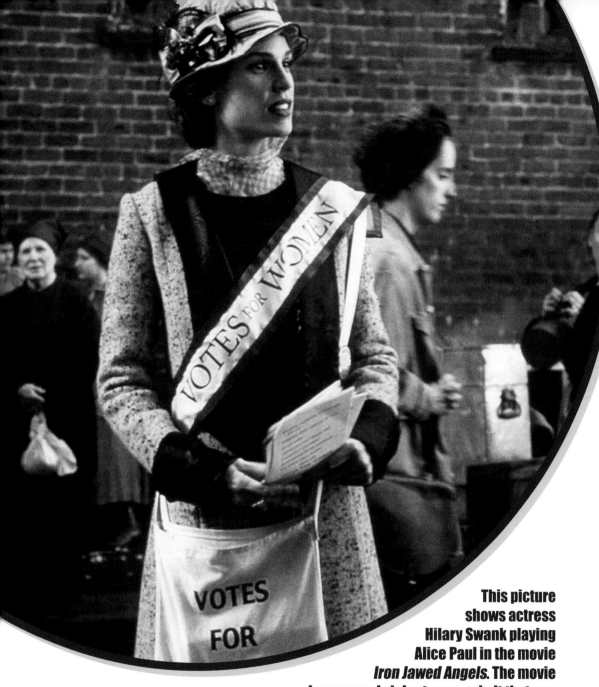

This picture
shows actress
Hilary Swank playing
Alice Paul in the movie
Iron Jawed Angels. The movie
has several violent scenes in it that can
be hard to watch because it shows exactly
how poorly the suffragettes were treated.

suffragettes realized they had to make themselves harder to ignore if they wanted to win their fight. Members of the group picketed the White House, which means they marched and stood outside while carrying signs.

In June 1917, police started arresting women who were picketing. Some were sentenced to up to six months in prison. While there, they were treated very badly. Some went on hunger strikes, in which they refused to eat while in prison. They were force-fed as a punishment. Force-feeding is unsafe and harmful to a person's body. Additionally, on November 15, 1917—which has become known as the "Night of Terror"—guards beat about 30 women who were in prison in Occoquan, Virginia.

By January 1918, a court had overturned all the women's sentences. The same month, President Woodrow Wilson declared his support for a women's suffrage amendment.

Fast Fact

Worldwide, more than half of all countries granted women the right to vote between 1893 and 1960. Some countries waited until much later. For example, women weren't allowed to vote in Saudi Arabia until 2011.

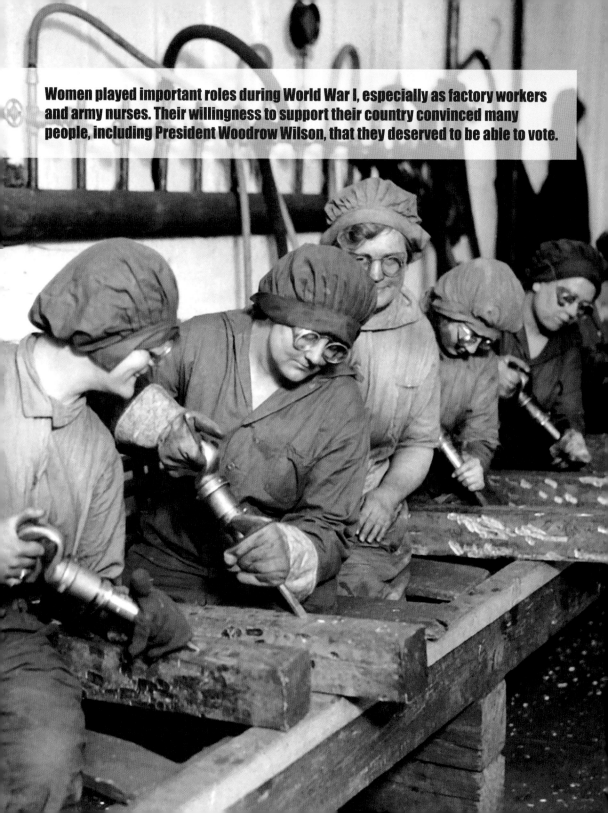

Women played important roles during World War I, especially as factory workers and army nurses. Their willingness to support their country convinced many people, including President Woodrow Wilson, that they deserved to be able to vote.

A GOAL ACHIEVED

All the work by countless suffragists finally paid off in the beginning of the 20th century. When World War I started in 1914, the women of the United States—including many suffragettes—played a huge role in keeping the country going during the war. Much of the opposition to women's suffrage broke down after the war ended in 1918.

Fast Fact

Although the 15th and 19th Amendments gave Black men and women the right to vote, they experienced voter suppression through unfair tests, fees, and violence. Black Americans didn't truly gain the freedom to vote until the Voting Rights Act of 1965 was passed.

In May 1919, the U.S. House of Representatives approved a constitutional amendment granting women the right to vote. The Senate approved it in June. It took about a year for enough states to ratify it, but on August 26, 1920, the 19th Amendment became law. The amendment says that all citizens of the United States have the right to vote. In practice, this gave the right to vote only to white and Black women.

THE TEMPERANCE MOVEMENT

Many suffragettes were also supporters of the temperance movement—a social movement to ban alcohol. In fact, some of them saw gaining the right to vote as a way to make that happen. For this reason, some people believe Prohibition—a 12-year period in American history when the sale of alcohol was illegal—happened because of women.

However, the truth of the matter is that women didn't have the political power to make Prohibition a reality. The 19th Amendment gave women the right to vote, but it was the 18th Amendment that created Prohibition. Male lawmakers were the ones who were responsible for banning alcohol.

Left Behind

Native American women worked hard toward women's suffrage; in fact, white suffragettes, who liked the idea of **matriarchal** Native American societies, often invited Native American women to speak at women's rights conferences. These speakers also talked about other civil rights issues affecting Native Americans, such as the government's broken **treaties**, but the white suffragettes generally ignored these topics. Despite their hard work, Native Americans of all genders were not legally allowed to vote until they were made American citizens in 1924.

Like Black and Native American women, Latinas faced problems when it came to voting. Many spoke and read only Spanish, so they

Gertrude Simmons Bonnin, also known as Zitkála-Šá, was a Yankton Sioux suffragette. When the 19th Amendment was ratified, she reminded white suffragettes that Native American women still were not American citizens and did not have the right to vote.

were kept away from the polls by tests that were given in English. Even after the Voting Rights Act of 1965 was passed, people who didn't speak English well—or at all—couldn't vote until the law was changed 10 years later to require ballots to be made available in more than just English.

Asian Americans had similar problems. The Chinese Exclusion Act of 1882 and the Immigration Act of 1924 banned almost all Asians from entering the United States and made it impossible for the ones who had already immigrated to become citizens. It wasn't until a law called the Magnuson Act was passed in 1943 that Chinese immigrants could work toward American citizenship. People from other Asian countries were allowed to become citizens, and therefore to vote, after the Immigration and Nationality Acts of 1952 and 1965 finally made it illegal to deny citizenship because of a person's race.

Voting Rights Today

The 19th Amendment was the single largest expansion of voting rights in U.S. history. In the years after its ratification, many women started running for public office. Today, women serve in many levels of government, from local city councils and school boards all the way up to vice president of the United States.

However, voter suppression is a growing problem in the 21st century. New laws were passed after the 2010 midterm elections,

After every major election, women place their "I Voted" stickers on Susan B. Anthony's gravestone in Rochester, New York, as a way of thanking her for her work.

two years after Barack Obama became the first Black president of the United States. These laws made it much harder for people of color, including women, to cast their vote. Voting rights activists have said that white women must be sure not to make the same mistakes the early suffragettes did and fight for all Americans to be able to easily exercise their right to vote.

FORMS OF VOTER SUPPRESSION

Rule or Action	Who Is Affected
requiring photo ID to vote	homeless people, Native Americans on some reservations, and others who can't afford or aren't allowed to get a photo ID
refusing to accept student IDs	students who are legally allowed to vote
no early voting	people who can't take time off work or school on Election Day
no voting by mail	the elderly, disabled, and others who have trouble leaving their house
closing polling places	people without cars who have trouble traveling to a farther polling place
exact signature match	people whose official registration has a misspelling and disabled or elderly people who have trouble writing
giving out false information, such as telling voters the wrong date of Election Day	anyone who is targeted (most frequently, Black voters)

This chart shows just a few ways votes are suppressed in the 21st century.

THINK ABOUT IT!

1. Why do you think women were historically given so few rights?

2. How did racism hold back the women's suffrage movement?

3. Why do you think the suffragettes were treated so harshly?

4. Do you think women are treated completely equally to men now that they have the right to vote?

GLOSSARY

activist: Someone who acts strongly in support of or against an issue.

agency: A person's ability to do something on their own.

appeal: In legal terms, bringing a case to a higher court for review.

debate: An event during which two people discuss or argue about a topic, often in front of an audience.

immigrant: A person who moves to a new country.

matriarchal: Relating to a type of society where women are mostly in charge.

militant: Using force or aggression to support a cause or beliefs.

oppressed: Harmed by a person's or government's abuse of power.

protest: A complaint, objection, or display of unwillingness or disapproval.

reform: To change something into an improved form or condition.

role: A part that someone has in a family, society, or other group.

stereotype: The act of unfairly believing that all people with a certain characteristic are the same.

treaty: A formal agreement between two groups of people.

voter suppression: Purposely making it hard or impossible for a certain group to vote.

Books

Dionne, Evette. *Lifting as We Climb: Black Women's Battle for the Ballot Box*. New York, NY: Viking, 2020.

Stanborough, Rebecca. *A Women's Suffrage Time Capsule: Artifacts of the Movement for Voting Rights*. North Mankato, MN: Capstone Press, 2021.

Wilkins, Veronica B. *Women's Suffrage Movement*. Minneapolis, MN: POGO, 2020.

Websites

BrainPOP: Women's Suffrage
www.brainpop.com/socialstudies/africanamericanhistory/womenssuffrage
Watch a video, take a quiz, and play games to learn more about women's suffrage.

National Geographic Kids: **Facts About the Suffragettes**
www.natgeokids.com/uk/discover/history/general-history/suffragettes-facts
Read more about the fight for women's suffrage and take a look at some historical photos.

National Parks Service: Women's History for Kids!
www.nps.gov/subjects/womenshistory/for-kids.htm
This website includes activities such as crafts, a word search, and a virtual scavenger hunt.